DOT MARKERS
ACTIVITY BOOK BIBLE

This book belongs to:

Palm Sunday

Noah's Ark

Altar

An
Amphora

Moses And
The Burning Bush

Melchior

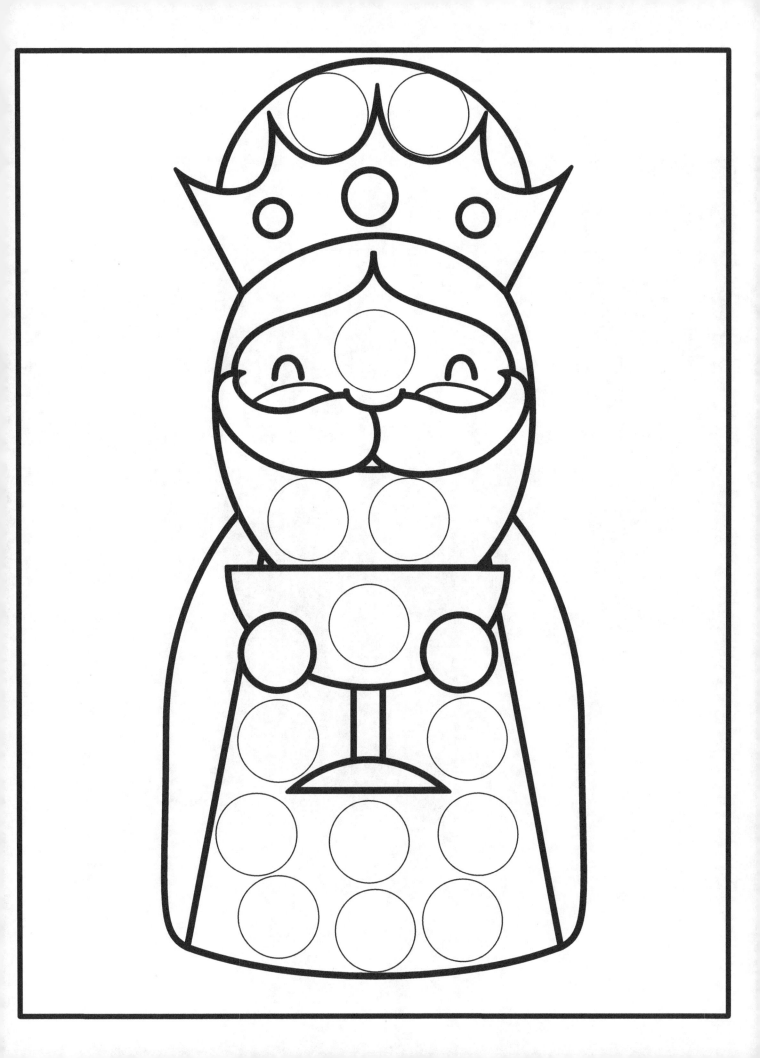

Gaspar

Balthazar

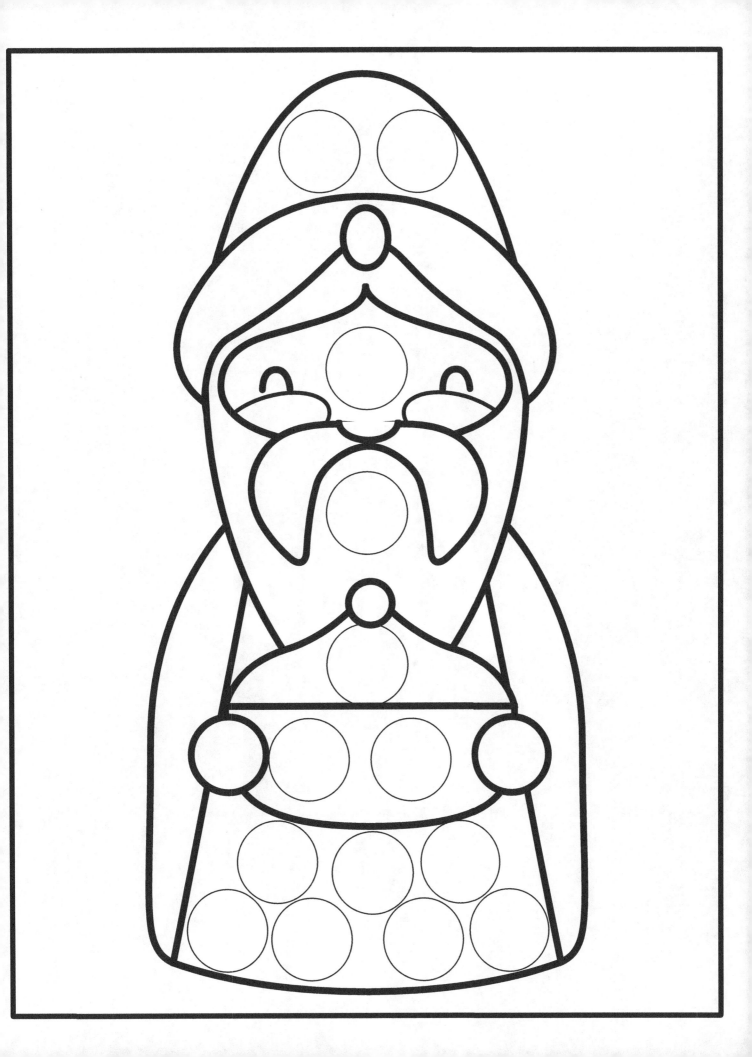

An
Angel

Joseph of Nazareth

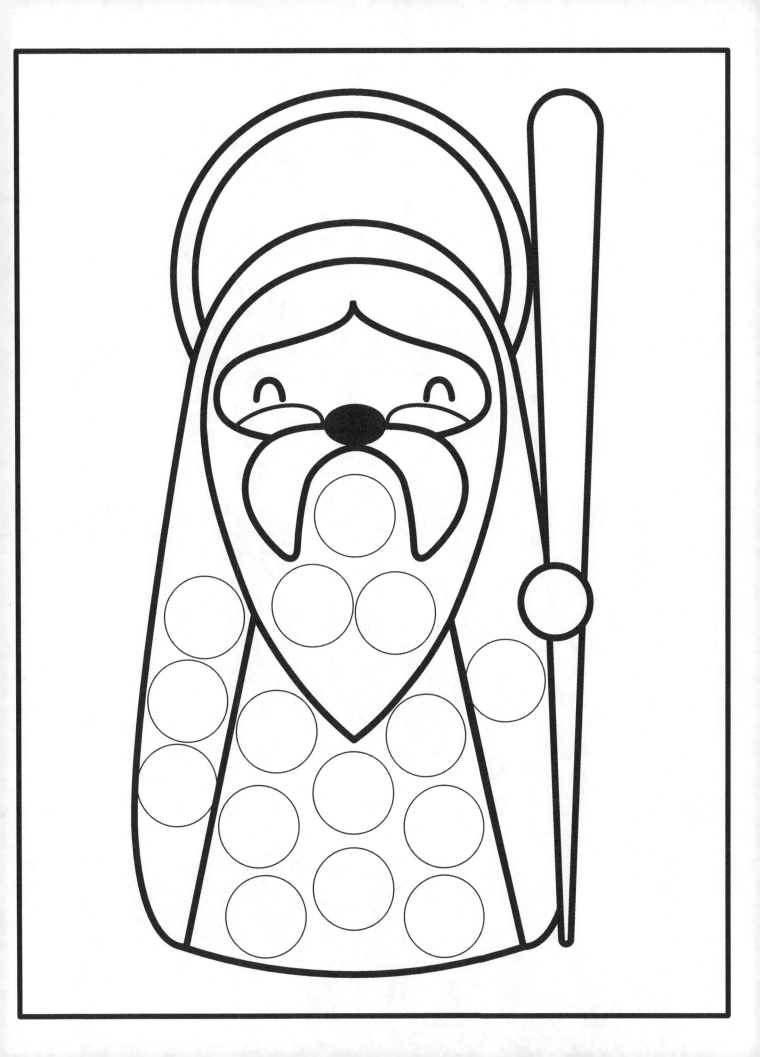

Mary
with
Jesus

A
Sheep

Ten Commandments

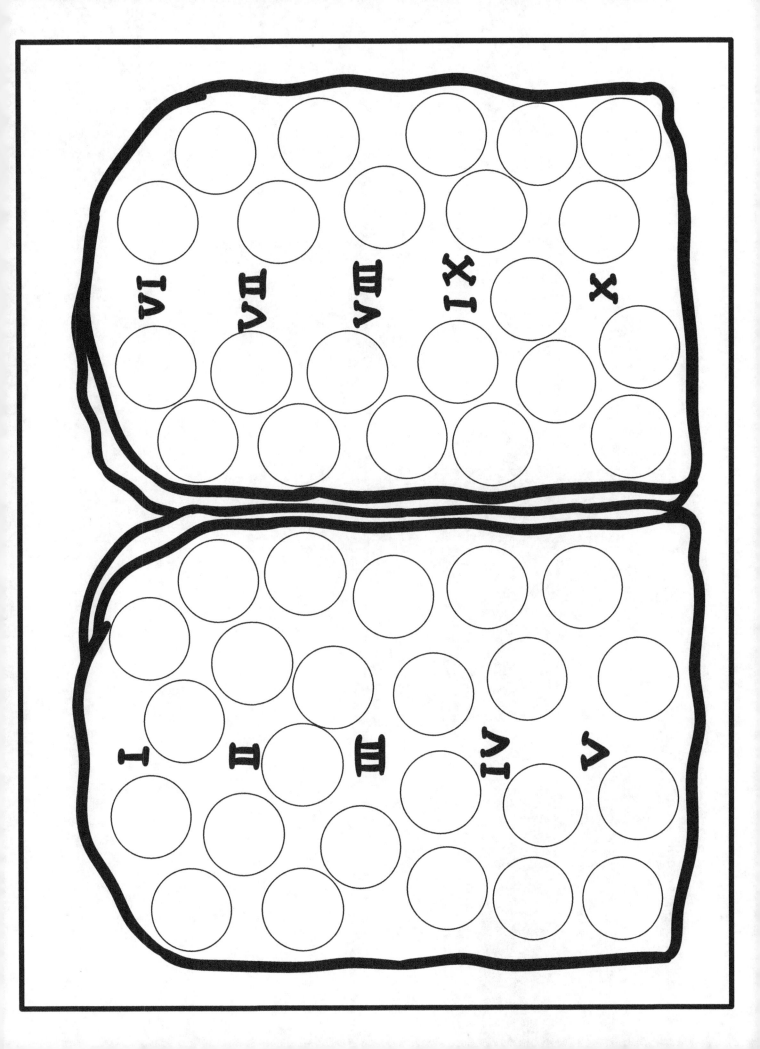

Amen

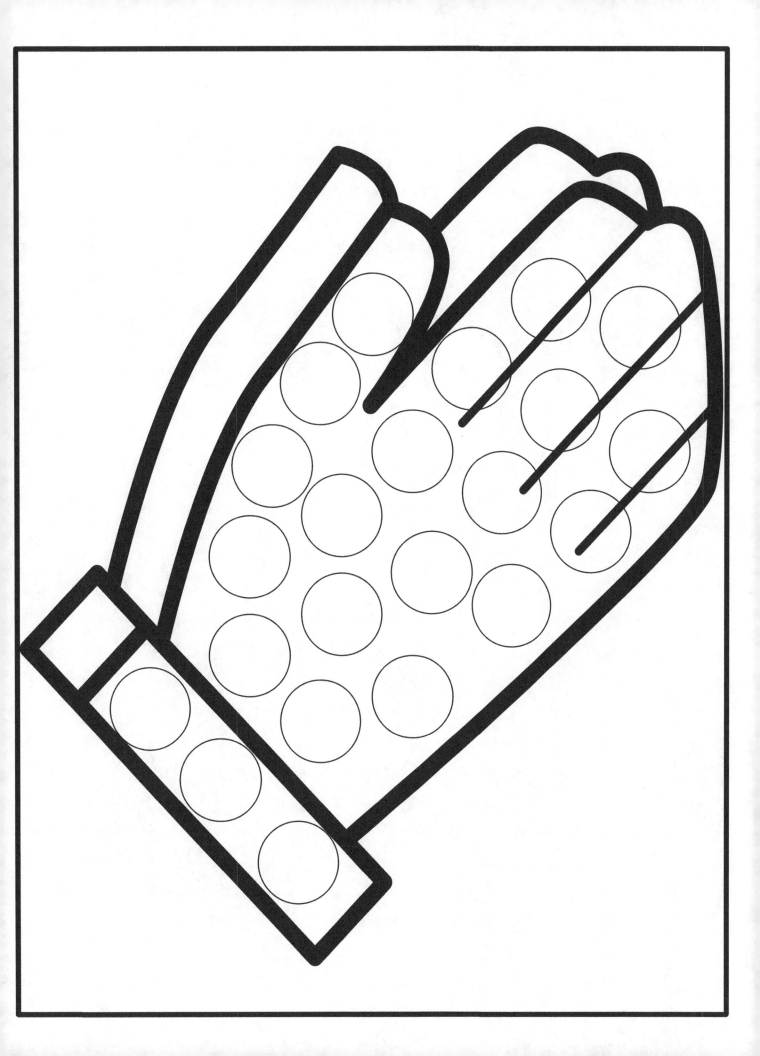

A Church

A Bible

Candles

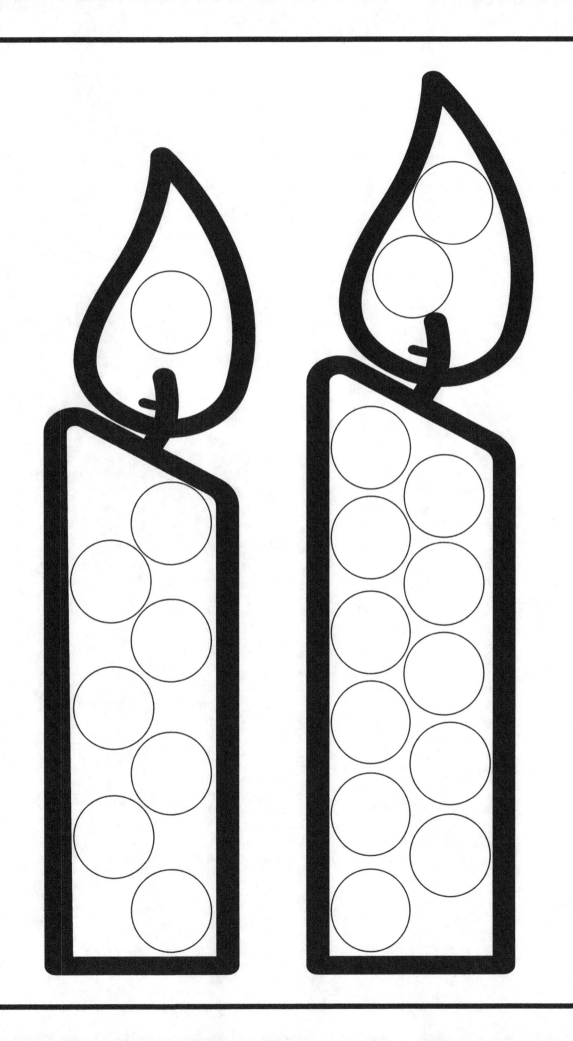

A Dove

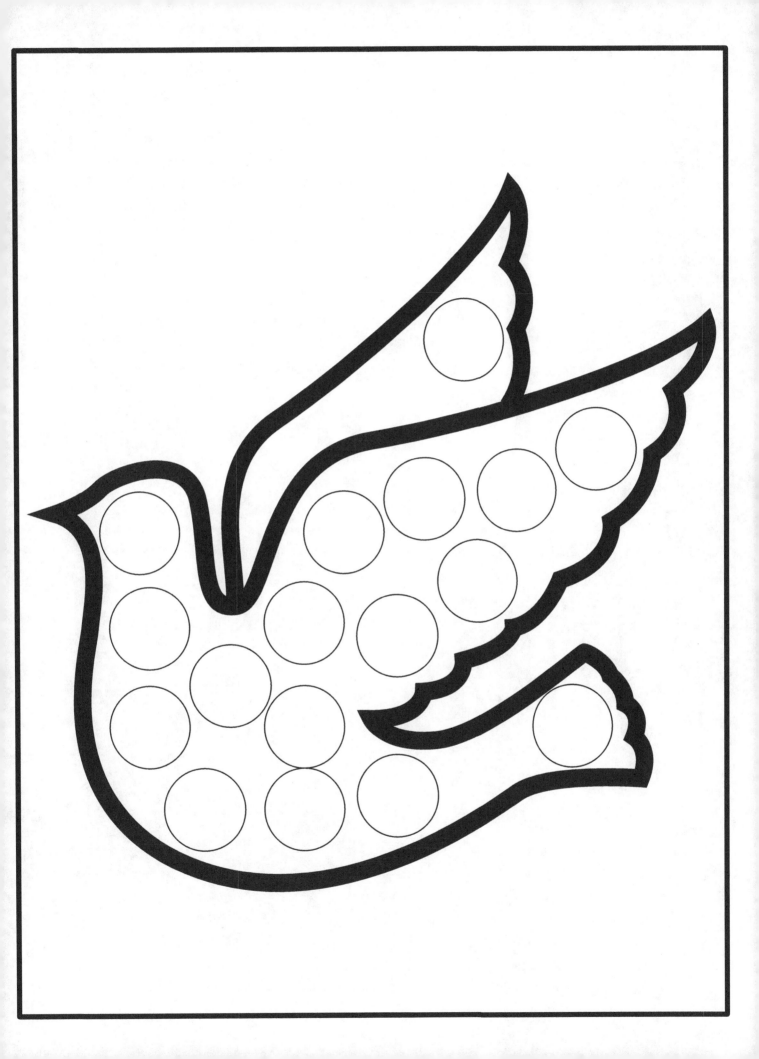

Cross

Washing the Feet

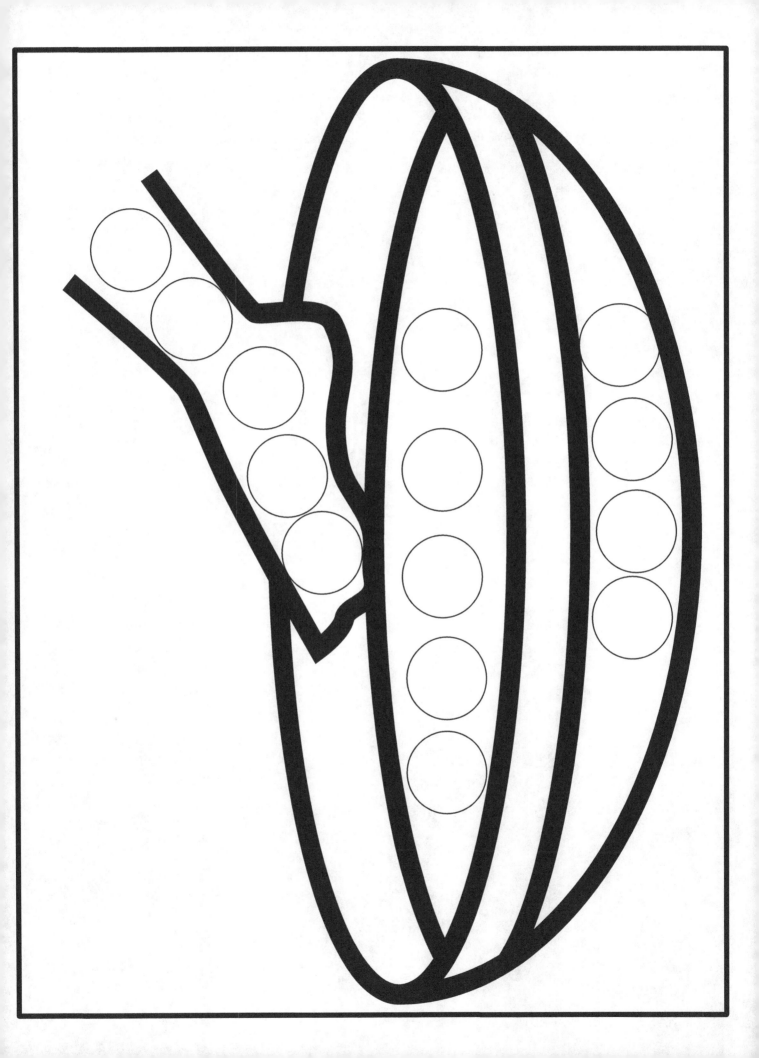

Stained Glass

Fish

Symbol

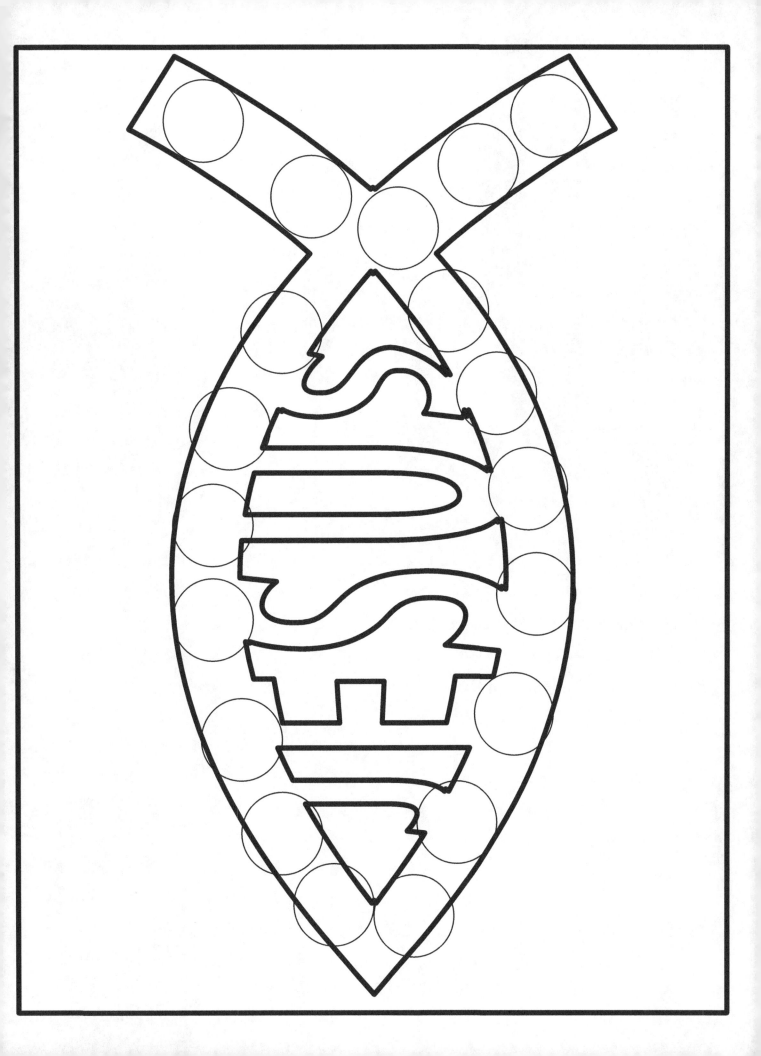

A Bell

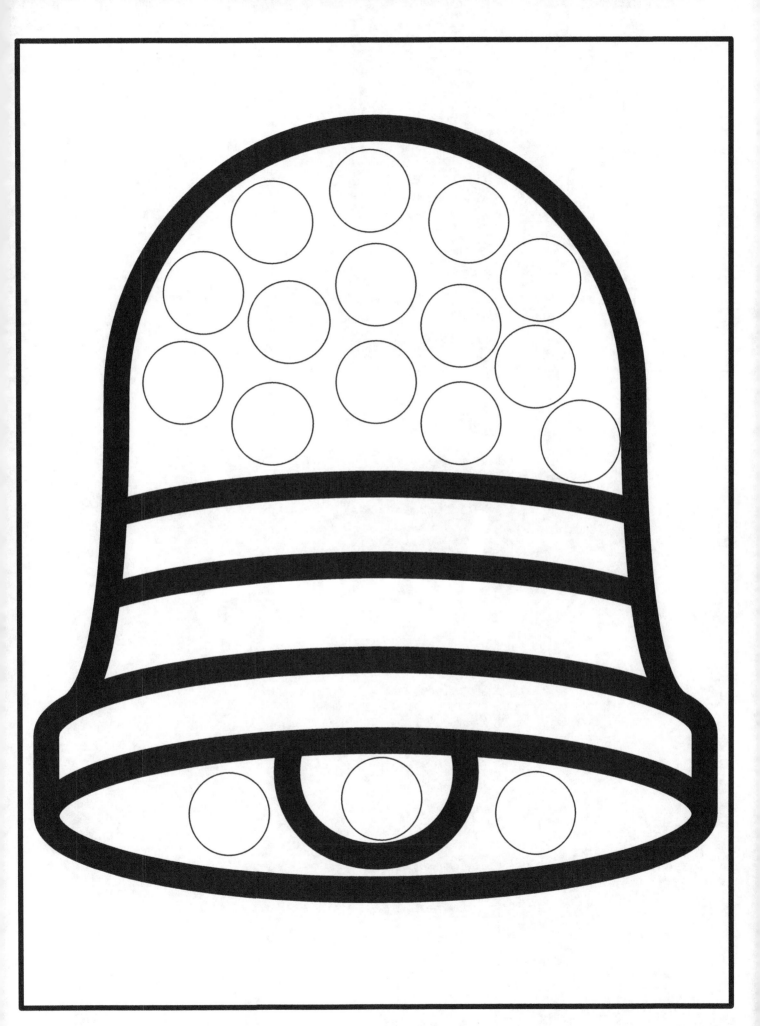

Baby Jesus

Last Supper

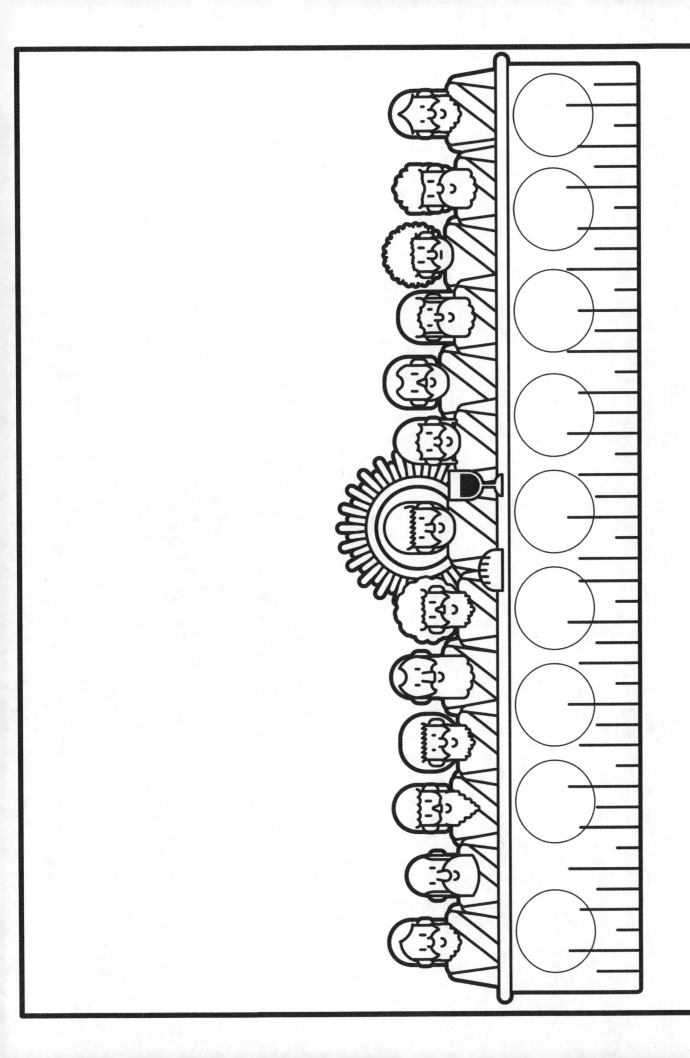

Crown of Thorns

A Bread

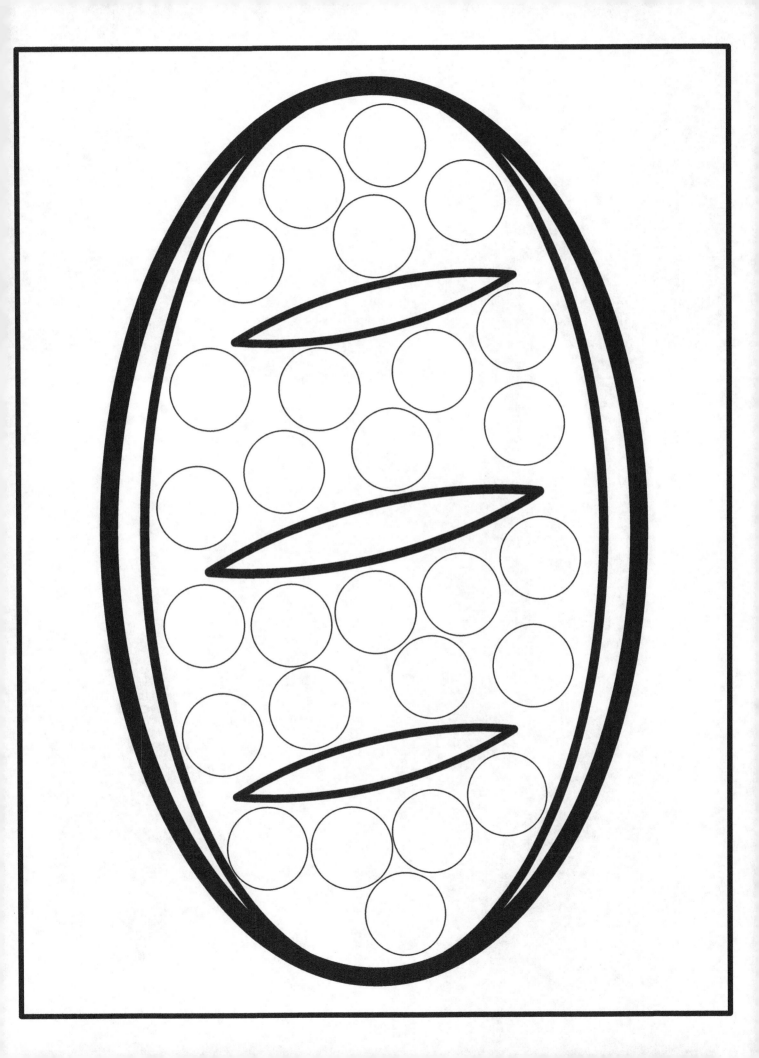

A Snake

An Empty Grave

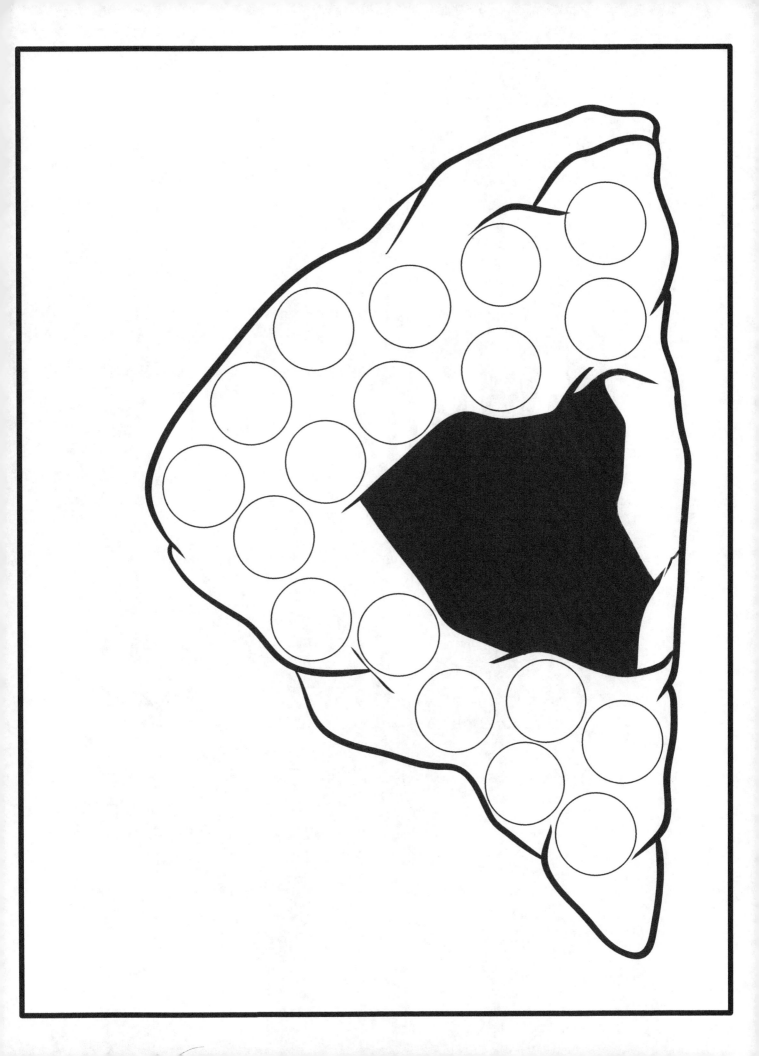

A Miracle

A Calvary

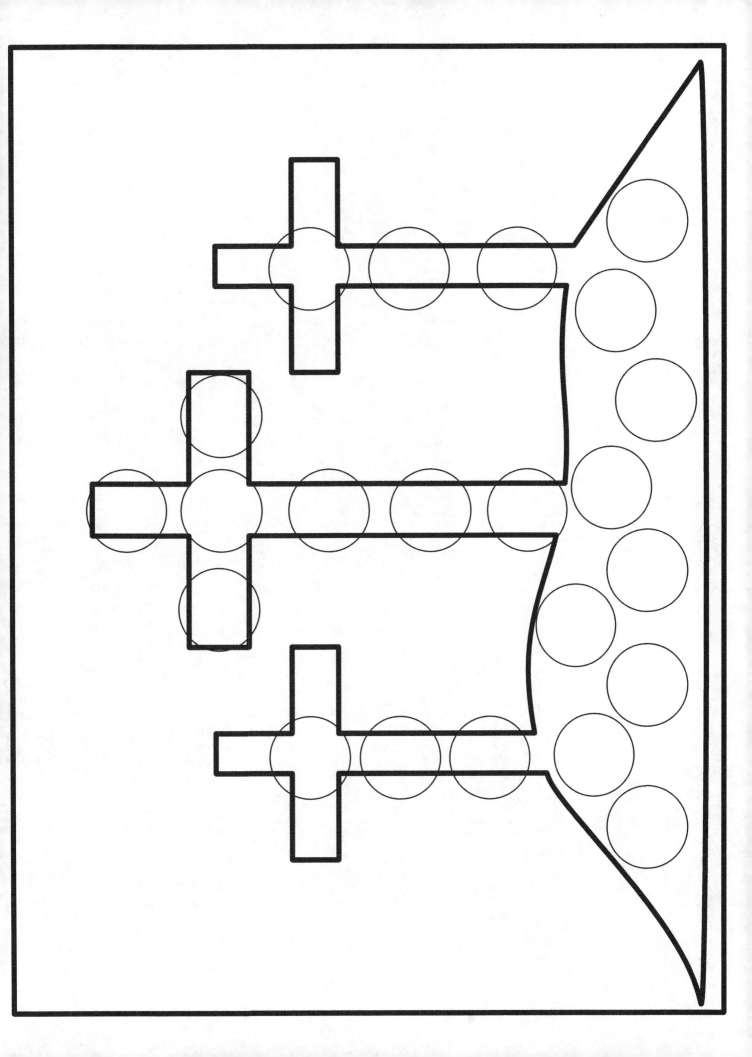

Made in the USA
Las Vegas, NV
22 October 2024

10283111R00037